ONCE UPON A DREAM

In The Land Of Dreams

Edited By Roseanna Caswell

First published in Great Britain in 2024 by:

YoungWriters — Est. 1991 —

Young Writers
Remus House
Coltsfoot Drive
Peterborough
PE2 9BF
Telephone: 01733 890066
Website: www.youngwriters.co.uk

FOREWORD

Welcome Reader, to a world of dreams.

For Young Writers' latest competition, we asked our writers to dig deep into their imagination and create a poem that paints a picture of what they dream of, whether it's a make-believe world full of wonder or their aspirations for the future.

The result is this collection of fantastic poetic verse that covers a whole host of different topics. Let your mind fly away with the fairies to explore the sweet joy of candy lands, join in with a game of fantasy football, or you may even catch a glimpse of a unicorn or another mythical creature. Beware though, because even dreamland has dark corners, so you may turn a page and walk into a nightmare!

Whereas the majority of our writers chose to stick to a free verse style, others gave themselves the challenge of other techniques such as acrostics and rhyming couplets.

Each piece in this collection shows the writers' dedication and imagination – we truly believe that seeing their work in print gives them a well-deserved boost of pride, and inspires them to keep writing, so we hope to see more of their work in the future!

CONTENTS

Oscar Polydorou (8)	106
Zahara Kachere (11)	107
Matilda Williams (8)	108
Harry Capper Wright (9)	109
Katherine Tanner-Morgan (9)	110
Max Heritage (10)	111
Indy Clegg (8)	112
Raphael Long (9)	113
Callum Paice (7)	114
Ellie Howarth (10)	115
Vismaya Vetheeswaran (7)	116
Hafsa Ahmed Bhatti (15)	117
Evelyn Thomas (10)	118
Hudson Henry (10)	119
Toby Conway (9)	120
Jole Capper (9)	121
Alexey Pavlov (8)	122
Mary-Grace Haynes (10)	123
Farrah Capper (7)	124
Samyuna Rai (10)	125
Prisha Ghattaora (11)	126
Kartik Kamble (9)	127
Martha Harwood (9)	128
Sanjana Parvathi (9)	129
Rhubarb Zahid (11)	130
Olivia Marsh (9)	131
Jack Van Clarke (9)	132
Reagan Dunne (8)	133
Noah Bowen (9)	134
Riva Li (8)	135
Jumaimah Nanteza (8)	136
Connah Seeley (10)	137
Selina Mkaya Jade Abdou (11)	138
Mia Pinto (7)	139
Isobel Adam (9)	140

THE POEMS

The Flying Dancer

As the clock struck 10 and the moon was high,
Through a dainty window, a tiny dancer did fly.

Her hair was golden and her dress as white as snow,
Her wings stretched out as her sparkling eyes glow.

Her face was friendly and filled with joy,
A welcoming sight for any girl or boy.

She floated and spun and then leapt through the air,
Her elegant tutu caught my glare.

As I arose from my bed and caught her grin,
Her hands reached out and took me up in a spin.

We moved through the air in a breathtaking way,
Glistening and floating, oh how I wish she could stay.

Suddenly, the sun hit my face and
my alarm began to ring,
I jumped up from my bed with a hop and a spring.

I looked at the window and saw it shut tight,
No flying dancer within my sight.

It was then I began to realise that it was all a dream,
The most magical dancer I had ever seen.

Evie Warrington (10)

Dream Of Saccharine

I had a dream of Candyland, oh, how sweet it was,
Where sugar spun dreams were crafted, and
candies danced and buzzed.
A world of sweet confections, that filled the air
with glee,
Where every step I took, left footprints on
fondant streets.
I wandered through a rainbow, in a land of
sugar treats,
Skittles paved the path I walked, a delightful,
crunchy beat.
Marshmallow clouds above my head, cotton candy
skies so blue,
In this realm of saccharine joy, my dreams could all
come true.

Gummy bears roamed freely, in a land so soft
and chewy,
Twirling their liquorice lassos, so vibrant, bright,
and groovy.
They leapt upon liquorice vines, as taffy butterflies
went by,
And jellybean birds, so fine, fluttered in the sugar sky.

I stumbled upon a treacle lake, shimmering with
caramel gleam,
Liquorice fish swam so gracefully, their tails
reflecting beam.
With a taste of chocolate-covered cherries, I dipped my
toes in bliss,
And as the caramel caressed my skin, I melted into a
sugary kiss.

The smell of freshly baked cookies wafted through
the air,
Sugarplum fairies twirled around, leaving trails of
powdered flair.

Lollipops stood tall and proud, like rainbow sentinels
so grand,
And gingerbread houses, so ornate, stood ready for
my command.
As I explored deeper into this saccharine domain,
I encountered a group of candy cane friends, full of joy
and sugar sustain.
Peppermint laughs filled the air, as we waltzed hand
in hand,
And crumbled icing snowflakes fell gently on our
enchanted land.

Caramel rivers flowed with delight, as caramel apples bobbed,
I dipped my fingers in the river, tasting the sweetness that globed.
In the distance, I spotted a chocolate waterfall, cascading with might,
Its velvety cascade of cocoa is a mesmerising, delectable sight.
Cupcake mountains reached for the sky, with icing peaks so grand,
Rainbow sprinkles covered the slopes, like confetti in a festive band.
I climbed those sugary heights, feeling frosting beneath my feet,
And with every step I took, my heart filled with a sugary beat.

I rode on a liquorice rollercoaster, twisting and turning in the air,
Giggling with delight, as my senses were swept away, unaware.
Cotton candy clouds encircled me, as I soared high and low,
My laughter soared, mingling with the sweetest aroma that did blow.

Cotton candy fairies danced in the sunlight, spun in a delicate thread,
Leaving trails of spun sugar wherever they tread.
They sprinkled sugar dust on leaves, turning them bright and sweet,
And dewdrops on petals glimmered like glistening candy treats.

Mermaids with peppermint tails swam in delight,
Their laughter echoed through the endless night.
Strange, peculiar creatures roamed around,
A candy cane rabbit, a giggling sound.
Liquorice snakes slithered through the air,
Gumdrops hopping, without care.

Sour patch meadows lined the countryside,
A burst of tangy flavour with every stride.
I picked them up one by one, and tasted their zest,
A zingy explosion, pure joy in my chest.

As the sun began to set, and the skies turned rosy, pink,
I bid farewell to Candyland, but not before I took one last sweet drink. Chocolate milkshake river, frothy and divine,
I took a sip of pure delight, knowing it would be the last time.

In the middle of my drink, I dropped my cup,
And realised that I had woken up!
The dawn light shone through the window,
As the ravens in the trees (not lollipops) began to crow.

I made my way towards the mirror,
And my eye was caught on the gumdrop (in my hair!)
that glimmered...

Hafsa Muhammad Nusair (13)

My Dream

I fell into bed like a shot bird from the sky.
I was just way too tired, I didn't know why
I couldn't even be bothered to get undressed for bed
As my pillow gently stroked my head.

I boarded the boat from the jetty
And I realised my hands were too sweaty.
The strong wind was making the sails flap like a bird
The noise from the sail was too loud
And my voice couldn't be heard.

At the start line, with 10 seconds to go,
When the buzzer went, I was going too slow.
But then I pulled my mainsheet in
And sped through the water, hoping to win.

There it was! The bright yellow mark
But look, circling it was a 20ft shark.
As I scared off the shark I tried to go round
But oh no, I ran aground.

Wait, there is a big wave coming
Hopefully, that gets me afloat. Yes! I did it.
I won the race and headed back to the jetty
My hands were no longer sweaty.

Aidan Holt (11)

Dreamer's Fright

The sun screamed yellow, trees glowed green
The atmosphere breezed calm and serene
The sky shone blue, clouds gleamed white
As a young girl, Amber, jumped with fright
Amber went towards the lion's cage
Just as they dashed and roared with rage
Their jaws opened wide and shut with a snap
While the crowd around her began to clap
Her hands stayed motionless by her side
The lions leapt and her eyes opened wide
The crowd cheered again, she tried to walk away
The teacher pulled her back and said, "It's okay"
Amber hated the zoo: full of creatures galore
She heard all the lions thunder some more
Her hands quivered steadily, growing with fear
She shivered and trembled and let out a tear
A girl in her class tripped her over and *boom*
She fell near the fence: the new place of doom
She got closer and closer, like an angel, she flew
She hit the fence and like magic went through
She landed, horrified, in the fierce lions' den
A shiver crept down her tense spine again

Trembles of fear fired through her veins
Her joy was lost, her hope had pains
Her smile was dead, her glee had failed
The frightened girl screamed, sobbed and wailed
The lions roared and made a loud, eerie groan
"Argh! Help, help! No! Leave me alone!"
Amber shook her head and opened her eyes
She lifted her hands and her head off her thighs
She looked over her desk and heard every laugh
She looked at the teacher, the pupils, the staff
"Dreaming, were we, Amber? Do not do that!"
The class laughed, pointed and started to chat
Amber's soul was embarrassed like never before
She hated them laughing, she chose to ignore
Her palms were pools of sticky, hot sweat
Her class kept laughing but she wished they'd forget
Her smile eventually grew back on her face
As she never gave a thought to that 'terrible' place.

Sienna Kaye (11)

Magical Creatures

Pegasus leap like a rainbow high in the sky
Dragons roar like lions in the manky, dark caves,
Unicorns paw at the emerald floor.
Sirens sing a song,
Click, clack, click, clack, go the elves.
Twinkle, twinkle go the fairies.
The dawn crackles like a piece of paper
In the fire

As the day rages through,
The animals burn and cry,
Neigh and whinny,
Wail and sing
And bears talk,
Goblins growl

As the night draws in,
The animals wave night-night to the beaming sun,
Dragons roar one last time.
Sirens blare their last notes.
All the animals
Enveloping the moon on a relaxing night.

Night fairies dance,
The goblins count the stocks
And the elves return to their homes.

Delighted guests,
Happy fairies,
Busy goblins,
Joking elves,
Wailing sirens,
Roaring dragons,
Beautiful pegasus
And twinkling unicorns
Gather for springtime ball.

The green leaves wave,
The sun smiles,
Fairies dance,
Goblins selling,
Elves laughing,
Sirens yodel
Dragons wail as loud as thunder,
Pegasus flying,
Unicorns gallop.
Everything is busy in the summer.

Gold and brown,
Yellow and orange,
Fairies chatter,
Goblins tidy,
Elves dance,
Sirens talk
Dragons breathe flames,
Pegasus gallops
Alongside unicorns.
Autumn takes its toll

The snow falls,
And fairies glide on ice,
Goblins sell shoes,
Elves play about,
Sirens sing carols,
Dragons hide from sight,
Pegasus stays away,
Unicorns toss and whinny.
Winter's falling, and the snow sows the floor in white.

Melody Lin (9)

The Golden Thread

I'm guided in by a golden thread,
As a world of fantasy fills my head,
I let my imagination float past Mars,
As I am transported to a world way past the stars.

I dream of a land, magic and serene,
A crystal lake, untouched and unseen,
I watch my curious reflection ripple,
With my imagination this big, I feel so little.

The whispering water runs upstream,
A bubble protecting my darling dream,
The forest listens to my immense secrets,
And the sun drains the sins of my demons.

And just when my time is about to end,
My curiosity walks me round a mystical bend,
And there waiting for me is my very own door,
Which will guard my dreams forever more.

As I take my last moment to say goodbye,
I keep myself a memory from the land in the sky,
And when my soul is back to bed asleep,
I wake the next day with my heart at peace.

Lila Coates (12)

Once Upon A Nightmare

I am in a nightmare
In the harsh glare of the darkness
My legs thudding on the empty
Space

I run, my head throbbing
I gasp, my heartbeat resounding
I cry, my tears rolling
Down my cheeks

I am confused
My senses bruised
I feel new wounds
Sprouting on my body

My brain is whirring
The cogs turning
No idea where I am,
I know nothing
Except that I am not alone

I can hear footsteps,
A monster is behind me
I imagine
Its hungry eyes
A deep bottomless abyss
As it finally corners
Me

I shiver as I turn around
My knees buckling
I make no sound
But somehow the silence
Is overpowering
So, so loud

I expect a hideous
Creature
Gruesome features
Repulsive
Traits
Catastrophic, antagonistic, destructive

But what I see
Causes me
To be drained of colour
Frozen, chilled, ashen

My reflection meets my petrified eyes
Her bloodstained lips
Curving into a macabre grin
I am gripped
By the urge to scream

Her eyes are searching
Lethal, brutal, fatal
Sunken and evil
How can this savage be me?

She inches closer
Victory is written on her face
As she licks her tainted lips

I shiver, disgusted
I crouch on the ground
My heart like a pounding
Drum
Thud! Thud! Thud!

I am in a nightmare
In the harsh glare of the darkness
My body, lying broken on the empty
Space.

Amirah Shafii (11)

In My Dream

I had a dream that I was walking through a forest,
The leaves were green because it was August!
The birds chorused,

In my dream, I walked through a wood of thickets,
I heard the gentle sound of many crickets,
I tried to avoid any mites,

The scene changed into autumnal colours,
I played in the dry, red leaves for hours,
But when I jumped I didn't come back down;
Did I have superpowers?

In my dream, I was floating above a world of white,
'Twas Christmas Day, this very night!
A dragon came and gave me such a fright,

In my dream, a dragon chased me across the globe,
I twisted and twirled, but was it too much of a probe,
Yes! A blast of fire lit up the night
Catching something on me alight;
As I fell, I saw the burnt part of me, my robes!

GeGe Scott (12)

As A Bird Goes Down

A flap of a wing,
Flash of white and brown,
That is all that you see as a bird goes down.
It was as free as the wind,
It was as fast as the breeze,
It was as happy as the sun,
It was as graceful as the clouds.
But now it is down.
Down,
Down,
Down.
Nothing, nobody, can save it now.

A flap of a wing,
Flash of black and fawn,
That is all that you see as a bird has gone.
It was as confined as a cage,
It was as tethered as a wall,
It was as scared as the dark,
It was as sorrowful as tears.
But now it is gone.

Gone,
Gone.
Gone.
Nothing, nobody, can free it from.

It will never be as free as the wind,
Never as fast as the breeze,
Never as happy as the sun,
Never as graceful as the clouds.

But it is free from the dreams that were keeping it awake.
Free from the false hope.
Free from the fall that would happen one day.
From the drop, the pain, the hit, the ache.
For now, the bird is free in a whole new way.
It is free from the grasp, from the chains of living.
It is a new bird, risen from the agony and ashes.

A flap of a wing,
A flash of bright, rainbow light,
That is all you see as this bird takes flight.
It is free from the cage,
Free from the chains,
Free from the sorrow,
Free from the pain.

For now, it is gone.
Gone,
Gone,
Gone.
Up in the sky where it belongs.

Iara Seaman (12)

Imagine This!

It's 2025 and imagine this,
The undiscovered are discovered
The unheard of are heard
The unknown is known

Marvellous innovations and creations are beheld
before us
But the power to create lies in the hands of a dreamer.
Dreams are the start of all journeys,
Everything that is or was begun with a dream,

A world built with your thoughts, fears and insecurities
Away from reality with only your emotions to keep
you company
In the delusion of a fantasy you lay lost in the bosom
of imagination.
The perfect collision of happiness and fears.
Unpredictable some may say, but in the depth of
your heart,
You are in denial of what is and could be...

You have the power to change the world if you take
the opportunity.

Folafoluwa Oginni (12)

Alone

There's a small feeling,
That's just not unpeeling.
Deep within me,
A lonely boat on the sea.

It's lost,
But not stranded.
In cold, stormy weather,
It's splintering and cracking,
That boat,
Well, it's me.

The waves are my peers,
Splashing about.
But I am so different,
I want to shout out.

But I will get bullied,
By all of the waves.
For just being me,
The lonely boat on the sea.

I'm being thrashed about,
By all of the currents.
Crashing at me,
The boat on the sea.

Their words are like seaweed,
Crusty and brown.
They're all over me,
Making me drown.

My mind is like clouds,
Ready to burst.
I don't understand,
What if I am cursed?

But then as I think,
Whilst I sink,
I'm just being me,
I don't want to be sea.

It's all the same,
And it's no one to blame,
It's just who they are,
The waves, I mean.
They're lost like me,
They want to be seen.

It is my chance to shine super bright,
To clear the eternal night.
I can be a big strong boat,
And even better,
I will float!

I can step out of where I am now,
It's time to move up,
And show the crowd,
That I am a boat,
A boat that can float!

And they are the sea,
A good friend to me.

Imogen Reading (9)

Solar Dreamland

The twinkle of the stars is in Dreamland
The gleam of the moon is in Dreamland
The dimly lit sky reminded me of coal.
The twinkle of the stars is in Dreamland
The gleam of the moon is in Dreamland,
Though being dark while now being light
The twinkle of the stars are ready to fight
The twinkle of the stars is in Dreamland
The gleam of the moon is in Dreamland,
Swoosh, goes the unicorn ready to fly
Shall I fly in this dream of a night?
Yes, I shall, my voices whisper
I am so excited to fly in the colourful solar system
Almost like flying in slime,
The twinkle of the stars is in Dreamland
The gleam of the moon is in Dreamland,
The colourful sight of happiness is tight,
What else will I see in Dreamland?

Kaiva Belewu (10)

I Thought I Was Going To Die On This Roller Coaster

I thought I was going to die on this roller coaster
I thought I was going to die on this roller coaster
My heart was racing and my body was filled with fear
The twists and turns, the drops and loops
Were causing panic, I could feel the tears

My hands were clenched onto the safety bar tight
As we ascended higher into the sky
The wind blew against my face, my hair
I couldn't help but let out a frightened sigh

All around me, people were screaming
But it was drowned out by the sound of my own
I closed my eyes, hoping it would soon be over
As we neared the peak of this terror zone

And then with a sudden and jolting jerk
We plummeted down, my stomach left behind
I couldn't help but let out a blood-curdling scream
As we twisted and turned, my sense of safety declined

My heart was in my throat, my body tense
This ride was an unpredictable beast
But as we reached the end, the brakes screeched
I realised I had survived, I had conquered this feast

I stumbled out of the cart, my legs shaky
But also with a sense of adrenaline rush
For though I thought I was going to die
I had survived, and that was enough

So here I stand, my heart still racing
But with a smile, for I faced my fear
On this roller coaster, I thought I was going to die
But now, I hold the triumph of being here.

Leo Prakash (13)

Once Upon A Dream

In the morning, I'd wake with the sun,
Golden rays kissing my face, one by one.
Birdsong would weave through the air,
A symphony of nature, beyond compare.

I'd stroll to a meadow, dew-kissed and green,
Where wildflowers bloom, a vibrant scene.
Butterflies would dance, their wings aflutter,
As if whispering secrets to each other.

Next, I'd board a cloud, as light as a feather,
Drifting across skies, wherever it'd tether.
I'd visit the moon, sip stardust tea,
And converse with constellations, wild and free.

Lunchtime would find me in an enchanted glade,
Feasting on laughter, with fairies as my aid.
Mushroom caps would serve as my table,
And fireflies would light up the fable.

Afternoon adventures would take me far,
To hidden caves and a wishing star.
I'd ride a comet, its tail ablaze,
Chasing dreams through a cosmic maze.

As twilight painted the canvas of the sky,
I'd meet a wise owl, with ancient eyes.
He'd share riddles and tales of old,
And I'd listen, spellbound, in the moon's gold.

Finally, under a quilt of twinkling stars,
I'd drift to sleep, carried by gentle guitars.
Dreams would weave their magic thread,
And I'd wake, knowing my heart was fed.

Oh, my dream day, a fantastical flight,
Where reality and imagination unite.
In this reverie, I'd find solace and play,
Forever cherishing my dream day.

Rabia Dar (11)

The Unicorn School

I dream of when I'm older,
I like to have my say,
I'm finally an adult,
And the kids go and play.

I'm going to be a teacher,
And go to teach my class,
I'll teach them all their spellings,
And let them play on the grass.

Did I mention something?
It's really, really cool,
Come try it out with me,
It's a unicorn school!

We'll ride along the rainbow,
We'll go and prance about,
I'll use the unicorn magic,
The kids can scream and shout.

I'll do what I like best,
To go somewhere and fly,
The wind will brush my face,
And we'll go up really high.

My unicorn has wings,
And colours of a rainbow,
She's beautiful and sweet,
And will even do a show.

The audience will cry out,
As we both go and pose,
We'll be joyful and happy,
As we line up in rows.

And with her beautiful voice,
We'll both cry out loud,
We'll sing amazing songs,
And throw sweets to the crowd.

Once our show is over,
We'll go and pack away,
We remember what we've done,
And think about the day.

We return to the school,
As it's time to go,
We lead the kids out,
And look, it starts to snow!

We all admit today,
What a perfect day we've had,
It's time to end the day,
To go home with Mum and Dad!

Ella Nicholls (8)

My Little Phoenix

My little phoenix has golden feathers
Which are as delicate as her angry tempers!
My little phoenix has sparkling feathers
Made out of soft golden leather!

When it's raining, her feathers go *drip, drip, drip...*
So, she rips them off and new ones come!

My little phoenix has a golden beak
Which always lets her speak to me!
My little phoenix lives in a golden cage,
No, not like a dragon! No, not in a cave!

Every day she sharpens her beak,
When creatures seek her,
She uses her pointy ferocious beak!

In a bad temper, she throws out a fire
Always when she calmly desires!

She is my best friend
And I always dream that we are partners!
Oh, my little phoenix!

Mehreen Mujeeb (8)

Once Upon A Dream

Once upon a twilit night,
I dreamed a dream that grasped me tight.

I dreamt that I wished upon
the seventh star that day,
And oh, that star had led me away!

It was azure and teal, and violet, and mint;
I remember light emerald, just a tint.

It shimmered and sparkled and bled into the sky:
I followed it yonder, through the corner of my eye.

It led me to a magical place,
Where the seventh star takes you is filled with grace.

It held breathtaking radiance and majestically
folded open...
Undoubtedly representing a fantasy curtain,
A curtain of beauty and nature, for certain.

Colourful birds danced in the air,
And in the distance, there lay my home on the range.
I gleefully galloped to the residence
My painted cottage will never change.

It thrives, not tilted, but topsy-turvy,
No wonder its dainty chimney is curvy.
Half a dozen daisies are scattered constructed
from candy!
One teensy munch leaves you feeling dandy.

I was feeling the bricks and smoothing the stone,
And then, all of a sudden, I sensed a moan.

I raised my hazel eyes to an orchid tree,
A fantasy novel and grassland were all I could see.
I flexed my palms to the sunset;
I thought: *my dream was too brief*,
Resumed my book, and turned leaf after leaf.

Aliza Mami (9)

The Power Of Writing

As I drifted off into a magical sleep,
I remembered a dream that emerged from the deep,
Floating upon a fluffy white cloud,
With bright blue skies,
Only I was allowed.

Far from the ground,
Not a person, not a sound,
Could move me from there,
Floating in the air.

At my desk, long, tall and thin,
I felt my imagination start to spin.
On my chair, I began to turn,
As my writing flare had just begun.

My pencil sparked with colourful light,
A story began to my delight,
A wonderful dragon rose to the sky,
Orange and dimpled, remarkably shy.

Wings flapping like the movement of trees,
Little antennas like bumblebees.
Off on a quest to save the princess,
From a dark and evil witch.

He swooped down gently to the witch's lair,
They both locked eyes with an evil stare.
They circled around preparing to duel,
The witch cast a spell with a crafty tool.

The dragon spat flames of silver and gold,
This greedy witch was easily sold.
She collected the treasure and to the dragon's delight,
The princess was free and she flew out of sight.

The moon disappeared and up rose the sun,
A powerful new story had just begun.
When I woke in the morning,
I felt power and might,
Because I knew in that moment,
I had learned how to write.

Marianna Gargaro (9)

Regret, Doubt

Dreams,
Dreams are just your imagination tampering with
your mind,
When you have a dream your perception goes blind,
Most dreams are directed to be just thought about,
My dreams are about regret and doubt,

As weeks pass, regret slowly floods back in,
The space in my brain is acutely thin,
Suddenly, all the regrets fill my consciousness,
No dreams are euphonious,

My whole mind grows silent,
These terrors are doubtful and violent,
Forcing anger, brutality and frustration,
Filling your entire imagination,

Kicking, screaming beating me to the ground,
Hurt, followed or abruptly drowned,
They're so bold, so vivid, leaving you gasping for air
Be awakened with fright, a perfusion of despair,

But the scary dreams are yet to come,
These dreams are not fun but tremendously glum,
These are the uncontrollable dreams that leave
you surprised,
You're stuck behind bars, you're paralysed,

You're bound by chains of shadowy fears,
Echoes of anguish will fill your ears,
You'll scream in silence, but no one can hear,
Caught in a nightmare's grip severe,

You'll long to wake, to break this spell,
But your limbs will betray you, you'll be trapped in hell.

Rupert Westwood (11)

A Spell Too Far

This is a dream where magic is real,
Where magic takes over and becomes surreal.
I find myself by the big oak tree,
Which looms and towers above me.

This is a dream where I am free,
Where I can control what happens to me.
It swallows me up and in I go.
Ready to brace whatever comes today,
Curiosity takes over and shows me the way.

Where I am, I cannot say.
As this is a dream where magic leads the way.
Unicorns and Pegasi soaring high in the skies,
And trolls and goblins with a million eyes.
Three witches crowded around a bubbling cauldron,
Wizards walking by with extreme caution.

Fairies and pixies chattering in the air,
Golden tulips and roses blooming everywhere.
I walk further, wizards and witches are buying
and selling.
Spells and potions and oh, what's that I'm smelling?
Boom!

Three witches are coughing and spluttering,
The cauldron's busy bubbling and everyone's running.

Where should I go? I do not know.
So, I run back, but I'm too slow
Green goo engulfs me so I stop and say,
"Someone help me, I don't know the way."

Fatimah Afsar (10)

Happy Dreams, Sad Dreams

Most of the time my dreams are happy, really lots
of fun
But sometimes my dreams are bad, and I feel
really glum
Some dreams are weird, others downright odd
I think the weirdest one was when I was a pea in a pod.
In some dreams, I feel like a dove
These ones are full to the brim with lots and lots of love

Some dreams are happy, some dreams are sad
But bad dreams aren't really that bad.
It's just your body storing away all those memory files
Instead of towering piles.
Your sad memories get you stressing
Or maybe not, I'm just guessing!

In some dreams, you're an astronaut travelling
into space
Or an explorer on their way to a mystical fantasy place
Dream or nightmare, your imaginary world is unique
I wish I could look inside your mind and have a
little peek!

Good dreams or bad dreams or anything in-between
Contain the story of your life, a life of discovering
the unseen,
So tonight, when you lay down your head in your nice
comfy bed
Don't be afraid of your dreams and remember what
I said!

Jennifer Rapley (9)

Being 12

Being 12 is fun
I feel more mature
I can be the older sister
But something isn't quite right
I can't jump around and be cute
I can't dance and scream at the top of my voice
'Cause I am the one to be mature...

As I look back at my younger self
I think of the times back then
The running around
The giggling
The easy work
No worries in the world
I don't need to care about things
Like school
And work
And studying
Things were simple back then
I thought things were sad when you trip over
But now it's about the constant worries that go inside
my head

Back then I had every friend in the world
Now friendships are complicated
I have more responsibility now
But I would do anything to go back to 4
'Cause back then I didn't care about how...
I looked
My hair
My outfit
And everything else
'Cause back then I was just me
And now anything can happen

Things matter more
But am I ready for these responsibilities
I think you know the answer
No!

Izzy Reeves (12)

At One

The girl was small, the trees were tall,
As she crawled beneath the leaves that fall.
A breath of wind blew through her hair,
She giggled and laughed without care.

She leaned against a tree, book in hand,
It was tall, gnarly, old but grand.
She placed the book upon the ground,
Then closed her eyes to hear nature's sound.

She sits in the forest with children of her own,
They make her cry and smile to see how much they've
grown.
They shout and they laugh, oblivious to the world,
They run around in circles, her boy and her girl.

But to everything special, there comes an end,
No time to say goodbye to family or friend.

Snow is falling, as death is calling.
Her hands were frozen and her feet were numb.
She collapsed to the floor, the Earth and her as one.

Her frozen tears turned to seeds,
Where new flowers grew,
She lay there in the forest, her life starting anew.
The noise of the forest was the singing of her voice.
She was at one with nature, like nature was her choice.

Isla Furness (11)

Marvellous Mars

Oh, I have a dream,
It is out of this world. I scream and beam
As I think about it. What's more,
Is that it is the number four
Planet away from the bright sunlight.
In the darkest night,
It glows in the sky
Very high.
It's a planet,
Red like a pomegranate.
I think your guess might
Have been Mars, which is right!

I wish that I could soar and explore,
As it has never been done before!
Also, Mars has two moons
That are like balloons,
They are both great helpers
And provide great shelters.
Even though it is dusty
And a little bit gusty,
It's a wonder Mars has the solar system's tallest peak
Called Olympus Mons which I would love to seek.

Despite space being desolate and silent,
Mars is the opposite because it is named after a violent
Roman god of war.
I'd love to walk along the rocky floor
So, my dream is to journey
I'm sure it will be worthy
To see the untouched planet called Mars,
Nestled amongst the stars.

Prisha Dash (9)

The Endless Door

Inside the brightly lit room,
With polished wooden floors,
Or maybe the lush, green flower fields
Featuring peaceful, buzzing meadows,
There was always a door in front of me.

No matter how many doors I go through,
Or how much the unique places change,
Nor if I found another way to leave,
The result was always the same,
There was always a door in front of me.

There may have been ancient, antique furniture
Or magnificent modern ones,
There may have been barriers along my way
And places I want to stay,
But I need to go on.
Therefore,
There was always a door in front of me.

The door is a devil,
That's what I thought of it,
But soon I had doubts.
The door sometimes took me to wondrous
Places or daring quests.
I soon began to realise
That the door may not be bad at all.
So, I began to travel doors
Continuing my journey,
So there was always a door in front of me.

Rayan Sharif (11)

My Holiday

I'm sat on the sofa wondering what to do
I know, I can book a holiday
And my friends can come too
Maybe we can go to a resort
That would be a very nice place to stay
Or maybe hire a yacht in Italy
What about a hotel in deepest Peru
Maybe somewhere that's got skyscrapers
That shine prettily
How about that place in Greece, it sounds quite new
We can go to La Sagrada Familia in Spain
Quick! I need to book something soon
This is such a pain
Maybe Japan, we can go tomorrow noon
What about Hawaii, where it is hot all day
Yes, but maybe India
They have got good curry
Wait, what about something on my birthday
The 23rd of May
I need to pick because I'm in a hurry
Fine, I think I've made a decision
I will pick somewhere near
Gosh, this is harder than what I saw in my vision

Oh, I think I'm going to shed a tear
Okay, I'm going to Cornwall and that's that!

Lottie Faith (11)

The Nature Sonnet

Nature is amazing when you look at it properly,
The smell and lush green leaves and the robbery,
Animals from far and wide came on a mission,
But one young toad was there in a jiffy, quick like
a flash,
He was known as Toaster Toad, full of lethal poison,
Trees had gone missing and with Toad on the
unusual case,
But Toad knew that it was his mortal enemy,
Headless Hen,
At Headless Hen's pen, he was plotting a plan,
One so mischievous, horrible and so very sly,
He was so engraved in his plan he never thought,
When Headless Hen had an idea a tree fell down
very near,
Suddenly, glass shattered everywhere, it was
slimy Toad!
He had come to save the day right on time,
An epic fight began, who would win?
But Hen died and Toad had won, or did he?
20 years later, old toad was in a soft bed,
As his last breath came, he said to his young
innocent child,

"Never give up..." dead.
Will his child be the next Toaster Toad?

Melody Robertson (9)

My Ocean, Large And Legendary

My ocean, large and legendary,
Contains dreamy illusions, enchanting and
extraordinary
With the twinkle of stars that reflect on the surface,
The ocean's magic unfolds a cosmic circus.

The huge beluga whale swam in the water vast,
Graceful movements, a ballet unsurpassed.
In the ocean deep, where mysteries dwell,
Its presence, a tale, its song a spell.

Baby sea otters danced in the waves,
Their dazzling gaze,
Staring back into your soul with glee,
As they have another friend to meet!

Water is sprayed from underneath,
Showering the creatures, keeping their coats neat!
The piranhas, so small and so vicious,
Are even too adorable to seem suspicious.

My ocean, large and legendary,
Contains dreamy illusions, enchanting and
extraordinary,
With the twinkle of stars that fade from the sky,
My cosmic circus bids goodbye.

Azka Bhatti (13)

My Nightmare

As Mama kissed me goodnight,
I looked out to the night sky.
I went to bed, hoping for a dream without dread,
Would soon pop up right in my head.
But I realised a minute later,
That my wishes did not really matter.
As I saw with horror that Count Dracula
Was in my room instead of Transylvania.
With his black hair, and with his pale skin,
His Sinister Highness
Could have easily been mistaken!
For Snow White the princess.
As he crept slowly towards my bed,
His mouth wide open, me like a sitting duck,
All I could find was a loaf of bread:
He bit that instead, and then his jaws were stuck.
A once scary scene was now hilarious,
I could not stop laughing, it was marvellous!
The next morning I woke up,
Still thinking about the night,
Even with a vampire,
It was not much of a fright.

Ladies and gentlemen, please forgive if my story,
Sounded more like comedy, instead of poetry!

Eleonore Ziegelmeyer (7)

Breakout

As I snuggled into bed,
Stories dancing round my head,
All those thoughts just floated away,
But then this strange dream came to stay.

As I woke up in my bed,
Looked out of the window full of dread,
I saw the whole town being wrecked,
By the monsters I usually kept.

They had broken out, full and free,
Running riot from the nursery,
When they weren't doing that,
They were crouching in corners, ready to attack!
I didn't know what to do,
It was like all my catastrophes had come true,
I knew I needed to help,
And I couldn't stand around and just yelp.

My eyes were wide open,
But I couldn't see,
Running without moving,
How could this be?

Now I blinked again,
This wasn't what it seemed,
Was this whole adventure,
All just a dream?

Zachary Potter (9)

School Sufferings

As I open the gates, a storm surrounds me.
Barbed wire traps the buildings.
It's like having to slaughter an animal
With your bare hands.
Rough rocks cover the cracked slabs
Blood drips from the trees.
Bruises all over my skin.
The world turns grey.
It's the worst part of my day.

I can taste the terrible treats
It's like you're in hell.
Shards of glass viciously stabbing me.
Chunks of blood ooze out of my skin.
As dark as death.
As wet as the sea.
No one can escape these deathly dungeons.

Dark surroundings cloak me.
Screaming trees, threatening shadows
Creeping up my gut, hitting my bones.
Sunlight barely hitting the gruely grass.
The trees are as tall as skyscrapers.

Eyes at the back of my head.
It's like a mirror maze but with no escape...

Priyah-Rose Kaur Guron (9)

Flying

Tumbling through the tenebrosity,
Glowing stars sweep the skies
A twisting whirlpool of rainbow petrol-like light
fills my eyes.
I was dreaming, was I not?
I fell, and fell, through a drain of dreams.
The sink to our mind,
The sink to our wit.

And for the land I 'twas in,
It was a pulchritudinous province, of foreign soil.
There were unicorns in the sky of twilight and
pigmented dust,
Their gleaming gold horns, feathered wings, flying
in the gust.
Marsh-like grass, spindly yet soft.
The sweet smell of candy shall waft.

Then I was thrust into the atmosphere,
The gravitational pull, capitulating my body to
the light air.
Pixies with hair so fair,

They carried me to the Portal of Dreams.
Away I went, to my world, away from sleep

Now away from dreams.

Naina Asopa (11)

Once Upon A Nightmare

Zshoop! Slosh! Flush!
I ran down the stairs in a rush
And there I found
Things that made a loud sound

Crash! Clang! Tumble!
There was a roarsome rumble
I tiptoed to the kitchen
I glanced, and then...

Wallop! Whoosh! Plop!
The hoover couldn't stop
The drier leapt and twirled
Whilst the washing machine swirled

Slam! Pschoo! Click!
The sink was filling up quickly
The toilet grimaced and grumbled
Down the TV tumbled

Beep! Gurgle! Tug!
I rapidly unplug
Quickly I run to the mains
Thinking that this is insane

Stamp! Whizz! Zap!
To my bedroom, I hurry back
Now nothing's lurking in my head
I can go back to bed.

Niamh Campbell (8)

Behind The Mind

Tucked up in bed, all cosy and warm
No sounds at all, no rain, no storm
I start to drift off and dream of a land
Where you can buy lollipops as big as your hand

And shooting down the road in a big black van
Comes a circus performer who looked a lot like my gran
I walk further along but only to see
A gang of pirates flying above me

They drop down the anchor and I climb aboard
Together we seek more treasure to hoard
Then out of nowhere, Santa appears
And gives me enough chocolate to last several years

He lets me on his magnificent sleigh
And with one shout, up, up and away
We fly past the moon and countless stars
But just as we begin to play, we find Mars

I hear a voice in the back of my head
That says I need to get out of my bed.

Aidan Campbell (11)

100 Days Of Peace

I dreamt of 100 days of peace,
Where conflicts and war finally ceased.
But when I opened my eyes and turned on the news,
All I could see was violence and abuse.
So, I pray that love will reach the sky,
And all the hate and anger will die.
I hope that my dream will come true.
Let's work together in unity,
To make my dream a reality.

We can live in harmony,
And have peace with all living beings.
Let's keep on hoping for a world
Free from fighting, violence and abuse forever.
Let's trap and chain all the hurt and pain.
And trade it for kindness every day.
Friends, let's not just look about,
We can come together as a community,
And be peacemakers.

Covenant Daniel (8)

My Best Friend

When I sleep I'm not alone
I have a friend that you might call Foe
But he isn't a scary Joe.

He brings me cups of water
But his skin treatment might be a horror.
He's red like a sore explorer.

He sings me back to sleep
With his wrinkly, holey feet.
And when he sings he sits on a very special seat.

He likes to eat
A very orange piece of meat
Covered in a fleet of fleas.

He has milky black eyes
That can hypnotise
When he sings lullabies.

He has long bony fingers
That are as soft as whiskers
And covered in blisters.

He could be a scary sight
In the middle of the night
But he's my friend
And his name is Schwend.

John Hawkins Diaz (11)

In My Imagination

In my deepest thoughts
When creativity is free
I find a realm in which reality is banished.

Every idea I have
Creates a new world
Where all of my hopes come true
And my heart is broken.

Because everything is possible in my world,
Even the impossibly useful,
When the stars align.

All kinds of creatures
Wander around happily
As my imagination relaxes
And transports me to unusual places

The vibrant colours are amazing.
Also, the sky is always blue.
What a magnificent picture.
As my fantasies keep getting worse

I see unicorns with wings and snakes that breathe fire. As my desire for all the unattainable things grows in my heart
In my imagination.

Michelle Evboifo (11)

The Deep Blue Sea

Beneath moonlit blankets, a dream took flight,
I leapt into the sea; oh, what a wonderful sight!
In the deepest depths, a beautiful story was told,
Graceful and intriguing creatures their limbs unfold.
They splashed and bubbled, they talked to me,
"How do you find it down here? Incredible, I see!"
There was a crimson squid as big as a bus,
And look, a dancing, wondrous octopus!
My heart was warmed, despite the chill of the sea,
I could never imagine something better, little
humble me.
Yet as I admired this out-of-the-world scene,
A sudden shake woke me from this oceanic dream.
Beams of sunlight shone, carrying me away,
It was a fresh morning, another new day!

Dorcas Yang (10)

Mission Venera 1

It's burning,
When am I returning?
I'm nearing Venus, who's frying my circuit,
Soon I may go into orbit,
I am in a spherical shape,
Is there any chance of escape?
I am done for, my communication is broken,
Czhh! Crackle! Someone is yet to have spoken,
This is turning into mission impossible,
How to make this possible?
Time to find and fix this communication error,
I have done it... I'm an excellent repairer,
I have started to study Venus' magnetic field,
What does it wield?
Hmm... interesting,
Is anyone hearing?
Finally, time to go back to Earth!
How much is my research worth?
Then I suddenly feel water sprinkled on my face,
It's Mom, I say, "Did I return from space?"

Aaditri Manjunath (10)

In My Dreams

Once upon a time, I was an angel,
Dressed in white from head to toe,
Living in a grand mansion,
With luxuries, I never know.

Sitting on the throne would be the heavenly king,
God, the Almighty with the elders' formation of a ring,
They cry, "Holy, holy, holy Lord God of Hosts,
The God who reigns but never boasts,
The God of yesterday, today, and tomorrow,
The God that can't be slain by Satan's arrow!"

Relaxing in the mansion would be me,
Looking back on my life and how foolish I could be,
I would look back down to the Earth
And watch over the mortals,
Wondering when we will come to defeat the beast.
Slice!

Chimno Nwafor (9)

Once Upon A Dream: A Dreamer's Quest

In my dreams, I fly so high,
Like a superhero up in the sky.
I zoom past stars and race with the light
In the dark darkness of the notorious night.

I meet dragons breathing fire bright,
And unicorns dancing in the moon's soft light.
I battle pirates with swords of gold,
In my dreams, I'm brave and bold.

But sometimes shadows loom and creep,
Monsters lurking, trying to make me weep.
I stand straight, with courage in my chest,
In my dreams, I face each test.

I dream of lands where magic flows
And endless adventures, nobody knows.
Once upon a dream, I roam and play
in my world of make-believe, where I'll always stay
I'll make it my own, like moulding clay.

Sehajbir Singh (9)

My Dreams

I see a light within me
A spark that's glowing inside
I feel so free
I tumble around
I am feeling pride

My biggest dream is finally here
Cartwheels, twists and flips
I look up at the crowd
And hope I do not slip

I love gymnastics, it's my biggest dream
I can't wait to start
I do my routine, finish and salute
I really did my part

A ten from a judge, another one
I really hope I win
I hear a scream from the crowd
I feel proud within

I'm so excited, I've just won
I'm jumping up and down
I love my trophy, it's big and gold
And in the shape of a crown.

Molly Williams (10)

Magical Land

I take a step forward, as nervous as can be,
But then I realise, no need to be nervous,
The strange land I can see is magical, you'll see.

There are rainbows and clouds,
And some unicorns scattered all around,
The strange land I can see is magical, you'll see.

I take another step, this time as fearless as can be,
I suddenly hear a noise, a unicorn is talking to me,
The strange land I can see is magical, you'll see.

So go ahead and join me through this magical land,
There is nothing to be afraid of,
Or frightened because the unicorns are here,
So stay positive and be you,
It's magical you'll see.

Caitlyn Bradley (9)

Dreams

D o you remember your wildest dreams? Nightmares, fantasies and evil schemes.

R eaching for the stars, no goal too high. Daydreamers do this often, watching endless time fly by.

E scaping from reality to the upbeat world of our imaginations. Dragons, centaurs, mermaids and your mind's especially exclusive creations.

A pples stuffed with poison, be careful what you eat, will this tart disturb my stomach or will it go down a treat?

M onsters wilting flowers, sucking out the life, extracting all the colour, striking like a knife.

S tirring in my slumber, so cosily I rest. What dreams are in store for me and which will be the best?

Elsie Vallis (10)

The Pond Of Wonders

The Pond of Wonders is a magical place,
Where deep down below you can see,
A tiny little fishy giving his tail a swishy.
And look!
He's coming to the surface!
With a jump and a swish and a flip, flap, flop,
When he goes back down there's a water drop!
A crystal clear water drop as round as a ball...

Deep down below you can see,
Your reflection!
"Hey look, it's me!"
With a jiggle and a dance and a hoppity, hop,
Down you drop into the Pond of Wonders.
Wading here and there and everywhere!
You look into the Pond of Wonders and you see,
A place of tranquillity,
Perfect for you and me...

Freya Goodall (10)

I Want To Use My Voice

I want to use my voice
To change the world because
Our future is important.
Speaking up will help all of us.

I want to use my voice
To save the animals
From danger and from suffering.
All creatures great and small.

I want to use my voice
To prevent global warming.
Icebergs melting, waters rising.
We must stop these things from happening.

I want to use my voice
To make sure no one fights in war.
I think this should be the last of it
We should have no more.

I want to use my voice
To make my dreams come true.
Then this will make peace on Earth
And this is for me and you.

Emilia Dixon (6)

A Dream Beyond The Border

A dream beyond the border
Is a dream out of this world
A dream beyond the border
Has been twisted and twirled
Though my dream beyond the border
May seem 'out of order'
But my dream isn't for me, it is for all
For those big and small, for those short and tall
For those shy, who get treated like a doll
I dream that each and every soul
Lives a life of bliss
Though sometimes life is the opposite of this
But dreams for me are like reality
An imagination sea, it grows on like a tree
With fresh, funky dreams, with radiant beams
Though that is my dream
My fantasy stream, my spark, my beam
My dream...

Aisha Mahmood (11)

The Eruption

The volcano has awoken from its long sleep
As I peek over the rocky crater
I see the molten lava rising
Just waiting to burst out

I hear it cackle and crackle
As if it's a ticking time bomb
But then the volcano erupts
As I jump on board
The searing hot gas
Scattered across the black-coated volcano
Making me slip and slide
Through the terrible smoke
All the way to the bottom

My heart was pumping
Faster than the speed of light
And my stomach was in a knot
I had made it down the volcano
And the sizzling boiling lava

The cat had got my tongue
As I had faced the music.

Juliet Ward (10)

Beyond The Gleaming Stars

Out in space, so vast and wide,
Were planets and galaxies reside,
There's a beauty that is hard to describe,
A million wonders in every stride.

The stars twinkle in the velvet night,
Shing so bright, a mesmerising sight,
the moon hangs low, a silver sphere,
Casting its glow for all to cheer.

The planets dance in perfect sync,
Following paths that never blink,
Each one unique in its design,
A marvel of nature, so divine.

So let's all gaze up at the sky above,
And gasp at the wonders we love,
For in this vast and endless space,
There's a beauty that we can never replace.

Khadijah Haque (10)

Power

In the dark, I cry myself to sleep
I try not to make a peep
Dreaming of magic and power
Trying not to tremble and cower
In my dreams, I was walking
And took a sharp inhale
As I was struck, a hurricane blew into me
And no one could even see
I'm trying really hard to stay
Instead, I can't, I run away
I run to a cliff and suddenly fall
To find that I'm not hurt at all
Every bone that I break
Suddenly heals and then I awake
I go to school in calm and peace
Then a familiar wind blasts into me
I run to the cliff and feel insane
Could this possibly be happening again?

Florence Burch (8)

Sweet Town

I dream of a magical place,
A magnificent magical sweet town,
Where everything is possible,
I sleep in a gingerbread palace
On a candyfloss mattress,
On the hillside beside the town
There is a vast volcano erupting golden honey,
Oozing and flowing into a heap at the bottom,
To the east side of the town,
You will find a forest of luxurious, cool lollipops
Dancing in the breeze,
There is a playground of fantastic flavoursome fudge,
Where I swing as high as the sky,
But I don't dream of chocolate spiders
Or marshmallow snakes
Because they are spooky and keep me awake!
I never want to wake from Sweet Town.

Elizabeth Bowden (9)

The Flying Boy

I went up to bed, all dark, all dark.
I went to sleep and saw a spark, a spark.
I stepped into the spark.
An air radiator flew me up so dark, so dark.
Swoop!
I swooped.
My eyes were on fire, what could I do?
I didn't step down, down, down,
Into my warm gown.
Roar!
What was that?
Roar!
What was that I heard?
It was a dragon who roared so loud.
I flew down, down, down,
To find my bed.
All safe and sound, resting my head.
No noise, no noise,
No other sounds.
All safe and sound,
With my mum around.

Alice Ford (9)

My Wonderful Horse And I

I had a dream, where I heard a little bird,
Oh, how my mind instantly blurred.
I followed the sound,
I looked around,
To my delight,
A creature arose from the night.
And it wasn't what I thought,
But instead, it was the neighs of a horse.
A colourful one too
With a beautiful mane, that flowed like silk,
It was as white as milk.
It reminded me of my toy,
Oh, it brought me so much joy.
We rode into the sunset.
I woke up and I was upset,
But the horse wasn't a dream.
I was relieved that he was right next to me.
And would always be...

Lul Nur (8)

Becoming An Ice Age Wolf

Gathering up tall to small
Are the creatures from the Ice Age,
I see them all
I close my eyes and then I'm dreaming
Back to the Ice Age, where everything is gleaming.

I wake gently in my dream, in a wet dripping cave
I am now a wolf, my feelings are alive and wild,
But I don't feel brave.
Other wolves are next to me,
Paws and noses piled up high.
As they woke, teeth bared,
The cave lit up with my horror and despair.

I took a deep breath
1, 2, 3
And I was back home,
Safe and warm in modern-day Canterbury.

Poppy Munro (9)

The Breeze Of The Beach

(Inspired by my love for the beaches of Pembrokeshire, Wales, UK)

The ocean waves say hello,
The sun shines on those who go,
To those who pass, meet the beach,
Relaxing and calm, flows the breeze.

Dolphins splash all day and long,
To those who sing happy songs,
To those who fall asleep calmly like a snail,
Wrapped in a shell, cosy and warm just like sand.

As the kids dig, they wake up their parents,
Just like that, pirates who sail find silver and gold,
As people leave, the sun goes down and
the moon comes up. When the stars twinkle,
creatures go down and slowly...
The breeze stops.

Haniyah Shahid Ali (7)

The Ebony Winter

In my dream, I was deep in Candyland,
Where distant hilltops looked like sheep,
Dozing in their cotton wool coats.
White plumes erupted with my every breath,
As the stormy winter breeze blew against my face.
It lifted the white blanket from the ground,
And covered me with a silky candyfloss.

Whistle, shriek, whine,
Not a beam of light in sight.
Zany children running here and there,
And snowballs flying everywhere.
Whistle, shriek, whine,
The leaf-greedy storm laid the tree bare,
While animals scuttled abruptly all around.

Mahee Ramessur (8)

My Shining Star

I looked up at the sky,
And I wondered why,
It was so high.
The reflective light,
Guides me at night,
And my star is ever
So bright!

I wish I could grab it really tight,
And wish to make the world better with all my might.
Sometimes I sleep and hope to wake up,
To a world where wars are made up,
Where poor people have food,
Clean water, and shelter,
And I pray that 2024 will be a belter!

Muslims, Christians,
Hindus and all faiths
Should unite,
To make this world peaceful,
Equal, and bright!

Aria Dani Leonce (7)

Lonely Cry Above The Lake

Perching on a high peak,
A sound in the twilight summons her.
Sweeping the cliffside with her tail,
She leaps into the air,
Spreading webbed wings,
The icy whirlwind engulfs her.

Soaring through the breeze,
The dragon flaps slowly,
Seeking the cry in the night.
Wind-borne and graceful,
Ascending into the heavens above.

She hears a yowl,
Abruptly startling her.
Reversing the course, folding her wings,
Her tail silently steers,
She drops into the sea below.
Diving urgently,
Splashing, searching.

Iris Kok-Roberto (11)

My Family Tree

It started with Bampy and now it's with me
The sweetest tradition of our family tree!
Each night, as I snuggle in my bed,
I'm always told a special story
That comes alive in my head
Will we think of time travel with dinosaurs?
Or travelling to space on our machines made
from waste?
All these stories of meeting and battling Pokémon,
Desert islands and never growing old
Are part of our tradition that is told
When I ask for one more snuggle and lie down in bed,
These stories become dreams, flying around in
my head!

Chester Morgan (7)

Flying In Tokyo

When I fall asleep every night
I imagine I'm in Tokyo
Vast, colourful blossoms sway in a blur
As I fly beneath the crowds
The moonlight shines and lights up the clean city
I gazed from Azabudi Hills
As beautiful birds elegantly glide past me
The people kindly wave at me
I wonder if I could live this life again
Clouds slowly pass by me
The temperature starts to freeze
I asked myself if I wanted to fly again and I said yes
Waking up soon, I wish I couldn't go
I'll be here soon, don't worry I'll be back.

Cara Tsang (9)

Amazing Women

These women are amazing,
These women changed the world,
These women inspired young people,
These women rocked the earth.

Frida Kahlo,
An injured woman with a big dream,
Who made it come to life.

These women are fantastic,
These women changed the world,
These women inspired young people,
These women rocked the earth.

Coco Chanel,
A young woman who loved to stand out,
Changed the lives of women for good.

These women are brilliant,
These women rocked the world...
And so will you.

Maddison Whittaker (11)

The Cuddly Owl

T his Monday night, I dreamt of my teddy,
E very night when I dream, this owl keeps me steady,
D own in the hallway, I pictured a thief,
D etermined, from my bed there flapped a great chief,
Y es, this little owlet, he bit and he battled,

B ewildered and bruised, the thief's worried teeth rattled,
E ek, he cried as he charged away
A nd never came back on a night or a day,
R unning, unlike his initial creep,
S o I smiled once more in my deep, sound sleep.

Harry Rosen (9)

Castles

In the deepest darkest parts
There are castles that break hearts.
But if you zoom out a little further
You'll see a castle of ecstasy.

Where nothing grows,
Not even a rose,
And nightmares start to row upstream.
Where broken hearts have shattered apart and lost.
Where the dream has failed
And hope is tossed.

But
A light so bright
Blinding the night.
A castle upon a hill shattered
And battered.

A castle to fix broken hearts,
There's a queen,
She's the sweetest dream.
Will save you from this labyrinthine.

Philippa Barratt (10)

Living The Dream

Messi, Ronaldo, Harry Kane
They're all people at the top of their game

But little me training each day
If I try hard I will turn out the same

Playing football at break with my friends
Hoping I get better when the days ends

I try hard at school in my lessons
But at home my dream is football sessions

Dream big, dream big, you never know
One day I could be playing down Anfield Road

Live every day like it's your last
With hard work, we can make our dreams come true.

Teddy Patterson (8)

Candy Land

Sleeping in a coma,
A dream to fulfil life's promise,
What a wonderful sight to see,
A planet full of dreams,

Flowers made of icing,
As soft as the candyfloss clouds,
Filling the edible fields,
With joy and happiness,

Following the candy cane forest,
With lovely gingerbread cities,
And lovely chocolate trees,

Until I slowly awoke,
The magical wonderland faded away,
Into the background of reality,
As I regained consciousness,
To see my loving family around me.

Isabelle Marziano-Doran (10)

I Dream The World Is A Happy Place

I dream the world is a happy place,
And everyone has a smile on their face.
Where no one feels the need to fight,
A place where people know what's wrong and right.
Where people don't bully or call others names,
Where everybody is included in everyone's games.
It doesn't matter the colour of your skin,
Whoever you are, you will always fit in.
A world where our beautiful creatures are safe
from harm,
Free from the threat of illegal firearms.
I dream the world is a happy place,
Full of wonder, joy and grace.

Jessica Ann McCartney (10)

Trapped

In the amusement park, in a humongous hall,
A maze full of mirrors, a labyrinth of sorts.
Some make my neck tall,
Some make my body short,
All these mirrors made me look warped.
I drifted onto a twisted route,
Unable to wake up, I felt trapped.
I was anxious, not knowing how to get out.
A familiar voice promised to save me from this horror.
I followed the voice until it said I was safe.
I looked up... but there was a mirror.
The unknown voice was me,
I had been tricked by myself.
I could not wake up!
I had to pick myself up!

Arthur Levy-Heidmann (8)

Doll Land

Me and my sister,
We have a very special land,
It's not made up it's real,
And sometimes gets out of hand!

We play with our dolls,
We have a load,
Five families,
All different and unique!

I like to make them all different clothes,
And Jemini brushes their hair,
I use my felt tips for hair dye,
I often have to share!

After a long day of playing,
We have to pack away,
But we'll be back tomorrow,
To play some more games!

Anni Patel (9)

The C Family

F amily is growing big and tall
A nd they were having a great big ball
M ixu, the dog, was barking away
I t began to snow throughout the day.
L ast thing they wanted was to be cold.
Y et the family were strong and they stayed bold.

L ove is what they always share.
O ccasionally they argued but they didn't care.
V ery brave superheroes never make mistakes.
E ven through the bad times their bond never breaks.

Amelia Clarke (8)

The Smelly Crazy Cat

I ain't scared of nothing
But I am scared of that
As it crept into the room,
That smelly crazy cat.

I checked the room
It wasn't here
I heard a high hiss
I felt cold fear.

I shook
I shivered
I pulled up the blind
I looked out the window
And what did I find?
That cheeky little black cat
Sneaking on my doormat.

I went downstairs,
And opened up the door
I shooed him away
And down the road, he soared!

Oscar Polydorou (8)

Nightmares

The thing about the dark is it hides my fears,
The thing about the dark is it puts me to tears.
Some say I fear everything,
I agree, I'm afraid of every eerie thing.

When you go to sleep,
You are trapped in a good or bad dream.
My nightmares continue to scare me,
I always wonder how true they must be.

I love dreams where villains take me to their lair,
And I fight for what's fair.
But with the good comes the bad,
And the bad makes me sad.

Zahara Kachere (11)

Italy

What I really, really want is to go to Italy
I've seen Gino cooking there on the TV

The meat looks very tasty
So simple with some rocket
Juicy, fatty, roasted, cured
Take the money from my pocket

On the beach, I'd dip my toe
In the clear blue ocean
Before I go in, Mum drags me back
And covers me in lotion

I wish, I pray, fingers crossed
I hope it's not a dream
Otherwise on my face
There will be no beam.

Matilda Williams (8)

The Gigglemouse

There's a rather odd animal
That lives around a tree, it flies
Like a butterfly, and buzzes like a bee

It rather likes honey and powdered rhino horn
But be careful, as it hates corn
If you offer it vegetables, it will simply cock its head
Offer it berries and it will ask for some bread

It looks like a mouse, ferret or shrew
But its wing outstretched looks like a shoe
Except for its vibrant pink
Which is why it was hunted, I think.

Harry Capper Wright (9)

The Magic Of Superpowers

In an alternative universe,
Where superpowers are part of this superverse.
Where being kind,
Is the right state of mind.
For if you are keen,
To be mean.
No reward will flow,
No magical aura glow.
But at school, the day had come,
To get our superpowers hum.
I was scared I was not kind enough,
But there was someone who was very mean and tough.
And they got none of the fun,
To play around in the magical sun.
But I got the top three luckily,
I hope everyone else wasn't that unlucky.

Katherine Tanner-Morgan (9)

Football Dream

I dream to be on the football team
To grow up tall and kick the ball

I play in the garden every day
Practising moves in my own way

I know it is not easy and I will not give in
Hard work and practice are where it begins

I love playing football with my friends on my team
We all work together and share the same dream

With every match, we get stronger and bolder
We dream of being professional when we get older.

Max Heritage (10)

The Future For Me

The future for me is hard to see,
But here's an idea of what I want to be...

I want to make things as beautiful as can be
I'm going to create lovely things for you and me.

I will design things you love,
From awesome dresses to stunning gloves.

With my creations, the colours you wear
Are a symbol of happy, angry and sad
And show who you are.

This will make me happy,
Almost as happy as you are!

Indy Clegg (8)

Nightmares

Fear and anxiety reign supreme
Take hold of me in my sleep and dreams
The frightening images of evil and gore
Left me numb but wait, there's more
The demons I saw, the bloody smell
The screams I heard, the darkened cell
It was all too real, this awful night
When I wake, there is fear and pain
I cannot move
I don't have a second to lose
Something moves through the trees
Can I get free?
This is all too scary.

Raphael Long (9)

The Dream Is Farming

I dream of farming in a wonderful land full of colour.
With a red tractor with eyes as shiny as emeralds,
Wheels as black as coal and an engine powerful like
a tank
The tractor works all day on the land,
And he looks after the animals
Preparing crops and feeding the people of the world
The fields are as bright as the sun when they are ready
to harvest
And the machines glow as they work through the night.
The dream is farming!

Callum Paice (7)

Mythical Creatures And Me

Last night I had a dream,
That everything was a theme.
Mythical creatures all around,
Fairies jumping up and down.
Night buses flying in the sky,
As the Centaur waves goodbye.
The fairies dance up in the sky,
Then I knew I needed to hide.
I went all around but it started to frost,
Then I knew I was getting lost.
I knew coming here was a bad idea,
So, I called a unicorn to get me out of here.
When I woke up it was just a dream,
And that it was nothing than it seemed.

Ellie Howarth (10)

Once Upon A Dream

Once I had a dream,
Me and Eddy went to the zoo,
This time Eddy had no instructor,
And he was allowed to feed all the animals,
So we went to feed the animals,
Then Eddy gave the wrong food,
And Eddy was nearly eaten by a crocodile,
So I said, "Time to get a snack"
(Whispers)
"If I tell Eddy we're going home
He will throw a tantrum!"
So we quickly went home,
So I shut Eddy in his room,
Then I relaxed in peace quietly.

Vismaya Vetheeswaran (7)

Love

It was a long time ago...
Yes, I still remember,
I couldn't let you go...

I was always quiet,
When you were around,
But comforted you,
Every time you frowned.

When we heard,
You had to leave,
I spoke not a word,
Cried for weeks.

You promised me,
You would make amends,
We would live happily,
Because no matter what...
You would come back again.

Hafsa Ahmed Bhatti (15)

That One Star

That one star,
A shining dot,
To illuminate a thousand galaxies,
Made to shine across the miles of black space,
That one shining star,
All that's needed to illuminate and penetrate
the darkest night,
It burns brighter than the rest,
Nothing is able to dim the glow,
Of that one star,
Not meant to be disturbed,
But left in peace and tranquil,
Forever,
That one star.

Evelyn Thomas (10)

Opposite Sides

Money, money it's just funny,
The rich don't care
But the poor need every penny spare,
The rich are always here,
But the poor slowly disappear,
They swim like sharks
While the poor can't eat anything in their path
We all watch time tick on deathwatch
While the rich get stacks
The poor break their backs.
Remember the rich don't care
But it's just too unfair.

Hudson Henry (10)

Dragon Police

I dream of having a dragon,
He will fly and be gone,
He will come back,
I will name him Zack.

He will be as gold as the sun,
I will teach him like a son,
He will learn about the law,
I want to be a police officer after all.

We will soar above the city,
Among the stars so pretty,
Keeping the peace in the streets below,
Making my happiness overflow.

Toby Conway (9)

Scaredy-Cat Gloves!

F ans were freezing in the crowd

O thers were singing very loud

O n the pitch, the goalie got ready

T he team got together nice and steady

B ut out of nowhere, the goalie's gloves shone!

A nd suddenly, *bam!* They were gone!

L ooking all over and everywhere

"L et us find these gloves," they shouted in despair.

Jole Capper (9)

Landscape

On the calm and relaxed seas bobbed a boat gently
As the wonderful trees swayed, a flying owl
hooted nearby
A group of speedy birds headed for the south quietly
This landscape is beautiful, breathtaking and
eye-catching

In this landscape
I see weird dead trees consuming the land
A gigantic factory sprayed out tons of smoke
This landscape makes my smile droop.

Alexey Pavlov (8)

I Dream Of Things

I dream of things
Like wizards and Willoughbys
And hot bottomed zilloughbys
Spiders and small spaces
Being attacked by shoelaces
Make-up and mermaids
And also beach spades
Christmas and carols
In summer, sandcastles
Boots and books
And lots of Starbucks
These make my dreams
And maybe yours too
So I dream of things
And so do you.

Mary-Grace Haynes (10)

Dinocorn Disco

Big scary dinocorns met on a volcano.
But something was wrong and they did not know.
So they checked up and down and all around
Wait! What was that? They heard a sound.
It was a triangle, and piano, then a trumpet
So they wagged their tails and started to thump it!
They danced together all night long.
Screaming and shouting their favourite song!

Farrah Capper (7)

The Faraway Land

The Faraway Land is a magical place
Where all the living things there will accept
your embrace
From a scuttling bug under the mud
To a great big bear whose cubs it will care
Big or small
It doesn't matter at all
Everyone is welcome to the Faraway Land
So off we go
Just take my hand
Hold on tight!
I see the light!

Samyuna Rai (10)

Dreams

D reaming of daisies soft and yellow,
R acing through worlds, feeling cool and mellow.
E very dream is different, stranger than the rest,
A ll are good fun; you'll think that some are best.
M y dreams don't last forever, but it's okay,
S o don't expect them to stay, because they need to go away.

Prisha Ghattaora (11)

The Dream Poem

Dragons, unicorns
People melting in sunbeams
You see all this in your dreams

Knights, soldiers
All their screams
You see all this in your dreams

Cats, mice, ants
Their squeaky little squeaks
You see all this in your dreams

Kings, queens
All their creams
You see all this in your dreams.

Kartik Kamble (9)

Dreams

D ream of a world of exploding volcanoes
R eal-life dragons with three scaly tails
E els that squirt ink as yellow as the sun
A glamorous princess prancing around a
M ajestic modern castle

O ctopuses with 50 tangled legs and
F unny flamingoes with floppy flippers.

Martha Harwood (9)

Once Upon A Dream

Once upon a dream
I could see a world
Of imagination for you and me

Once upon a dream
I could see a pathway
Beyond the deep, blue sea

Once upon a dream
I could see a box
Of imagination with a key

Once upon a dream
I could see a world
Of imagination for you and me.

Sanjana Parvathi (9)

The Dream Of Camping

Once upon a dream, I went,
Imagining myself camping in a tent,
With shooting stars that soar
Across the sky
Under them is where we lie
Around the fire, we toast marshmallows
And eat them with glee,
Because over here,
Our imaginations run free,
With no limits or boundaries.

Rhubarb Zahid (11)

All About Dreams

D reams are the worlds you choose

R ight or wrong doesn't occur in dreams

E njoy your dreams as long as they last

A chieve your dreams then share them with everyone

M ore and more happiness is awaiting in the future

S o enjoy before you reach the end.

Olivia Marsh (9)

The Day The Sun Collapsed

It was like a raging fire burning bright
In the middle of the night
The sun didn't want us to have fun
So he went close to the Earth
And burnt our turf
Then the moon came and told the sun
Not to make life lame
And then swung him back to his place
In the middle of space.

Jack Van Clarke (9)

On My Way To Dublin

On the plane
Looking out the window
With my family having fun
Making this poem makes my day
Up high in the sky
Oh my, not it's night

Only 190 minutes until we land
Oh look, I can see the sand
My dream is to go to the beach
The beach is within reach.

Reagan Dunne (8)

Historical Dreams

Dirty, dark, crowded,
Rats, disease punishing lives,
Humiliation.

Toxic blood and water,
Rye bread, vegetables and gravy,
Pelting rotten food.

Pickpocketing life,
Child labour, up chimneys,
Carrying gunpowder.

Noah Bowen (9)

Knight

Once upon a time
There was a knight
Who kept his armour shiny and bright
Every time
Before a fight
He'd paint his eyebrows ghostly white
He also had a snake
Which would
Always give its victim a nasty fright.

Riva Li (8)

Dreams

Dreams are wonderful things,
They take you on a journey
Where anything is possible.

Some dreams have unicorns,
Others have dinosaurs.
Even if your dream has a bird that caws,
You know it's truly yours.

Jumaimah Nanteza (8)

Cats

Cats sit on mats,
And dream about rats.

Cats have long tails,
And have claws, not nails.

Our cat drinks from taps,
And sits on our laps.

Our cat has spotty fur,
And we love her!

Connah Seeley (10)

Dreams Smell Like Almonds

Haikus

Almond-smelling news,
Dance to a wonderful tune.
My heart longs for June.

Fame's prophecy meant,
There were many hands to hold,
And it cured my cold.

(So I belong in Busan).

Selina Mkaya Jade Abdou (11)

Vikings

V icious times
I ce-cold seas
K ings are powerful
I am brave
N othing can stop me
G ot this
S inging in Valhalla.

Mia Pinto (7)

Me

My imagination
Fun, crazy
Imaginative, creative, joyful
A world of joy
Tranquil, jovial, gleeful
Perpetual, superior
Inside my mind.

Isobel Adam (9)

YoungWriters®
— Est. 1991 —

YOUNG WRITERS
INFORMATION

We hope you have enjoyed reading this book – and
that you will continue to in the coming years.

If you're a young writer who enjoys reading and creative writing,
or the parent of an enthusiastic poet or story writer,
do visit our website **www.youngwriters.co.uk**. Here you will
find free competitions, workshops and games, as well as
recommended reads, a poetry glossary and our blog.

If you would like to order further copies of this book,
or any of our other titles, then please give us a
call or visit **www.youngwriters.co.uk**.

Young Writers
Remus House
Coltsfoot Drive
Peterborough
PE2 9BF
(01733) 890066
info@youngwriters.co.uk

f YoungWritersUK **✗** YoungWritersCW
◉ youngwriterscw **♪** youngwriterscw